SETTING YOUR SIGHTS ON THE INTERSECTION

90-DAY
DEVOTIONAL & JOURNAL

Setting Your Sights on the Intersection

90-Day Devotional & Journal

INTERSECTION

Where God's Wealth Meets God's Wisdom

JOHNNY MCWILLIAMS

Zero In Financial Press

Myrtle Beach, South Carolina

Zero In Financial Press
PO BOX 1718
Myrtle Beach, SC 29578
United States of America

Full Disclosure: Some of the links in this book and related materials may be affiliate links (excluding any and all links to Amazon), and we may earn a small commission when you make a purchase through them, at no additional cost to you. By FTC law we must disclose this. However, we want to assure you that we only endorse products and services we believe in and would or do use ourselves.

Setting Your Sights on the Intersection, 90-Day Devotional & Journal / Series: INTERSECTION, Where God's Wealth Meets God's Wisdom / Johnny McWilliams, author.

Hardback ISBN-13: 978-1-954485-21-1
Paperback ISBN-13: 978-1-954485-20-4
E-book (PDF) ISBN-13: 978-1-954485-22-8

Access free resources mentioned in this book:
intersection.zeroinfinancial.com

Editor: Fleur Marie Vaz, fleurmarievaz@gmail.com
Additional Editing: Melanie Brown
Cover image design: Edgar Rios, edgrrr5@gmail.com

Contents

… with readings from INTERSECTION: *Biblical Faith Meet Financial Strategy — How to Lay a Solid Foundation for Prosperity.*

… with readings from INTERSECTION: *God's Ownership Meets Money Management — How to Be a Good and Faithful Steward.*

… with readings from INTERSECTION: *Divine Provision Meets Generosity Planning — How to Live Life to the Fullest While Richly Giving.*

Dedication

I dedicate this book series to my Lord and Savior, Jesus Christ, who has carried me, walked with me, and led me all the way to completion. Thank You for always being the God who always keeps His promises.

> *And the Lord, he it is that doth go before thee; he will be with thee, he will not fail thee, neither forsake thee: fear not, neither be dismayed (Deuteronomy 31:8).*

Acknowledgments

I want to acknowledge and thank my best friend and incredible wife, Christine. Your undying support never ceases to amaze me. You have stood by me through it all. I couldn't have finished this project without you.

Thank you to my children, Seth and Paige. I love you and am so proud to be your dad. Your faith in Christ and success in life have been a beautiful display of God's grace.

Thank you to my parents, Clovers and Val McWilliams. You have always been a rock of consistent encouragement, believing in me throughout the decades. You both have faithfully studied the Word of God and have inspired me to do the same. Your prayers have kept blessings pouring out upon my life.

Thank you to my Pastor for over a decade, Al Toledo, for your powerful teaching and ministry that will always have a lasting influence on my business and writing. And to my current Pastor, Chris Honeycutt, who has been abundantly supportive as I worked through the last twelve months of this project.

Free Resources

To help you Zero In on the INTERSECTION where God's Wealth meets God's Wisdom, download the free resources from the INTERSECTION Resource Page:

intersection.zeroinfinancial.com

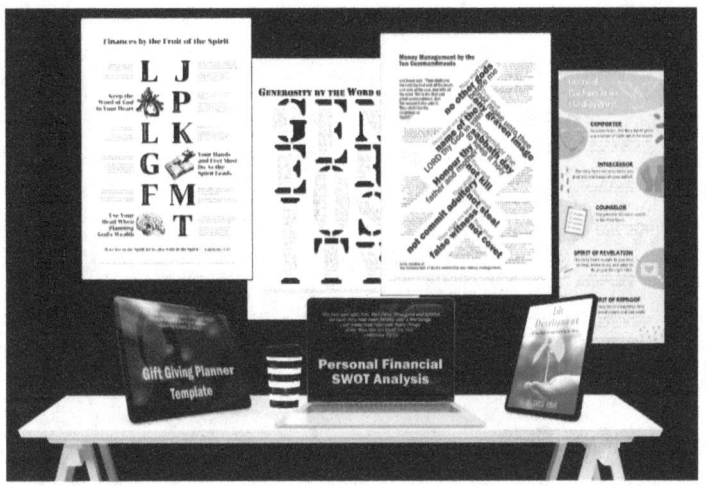

- **BOOK:** Life Development—A New Believer's Guide to Growing in Christ

- **INFOGRAPHIC:** Financial Guidance from the Holy Spirit

- **POSTER:** Finances by the Fruit of the Spirit

- **WORKBOOK:** Personal Financial SWOT Analysis

- **POSTER:** Money Management by the Ten Commandments

- **WORKBOOK:** Gift Giving Planner Template

- **POSTER:** Generosity by the Word of God

INTRODUCTION

Ready. Aim. Focus.

Are you ready to zero in on your financial target? The first step is to set your sights on the intersection.

Welcome to the 90-Day Devotional & Journal that will lead you through the book series *INTERSECTION — Where God's Wealth Meets God's Wisdom.* This guide will walk with you as you read book by book, part by part, chapter by chapter, and section by section. You will spend three days in each of the 30 chapters. The readings will vary by length, but the average reader will be able to complete each selection in thirty minutes or less.

Along with each daily reading, there will be one key Bible verse to meditate on and do further research on if you wish. There will be 2-4 questions to help you search out the scripture and go deeper. Finally, there will be journal prompts, which are suggestions to guide your personal writings and reflections. Don't let any of this limit your prayers and thoughts on the day's teachings, instead allow them to give you a starting point as the Holy Spirit does His work in you.

If you don't have the book to follow along with the corresponding reading, don't worry, you can still get a lot out of studying the scripture, answering the questions, and considering the journal prompts. To get the most out of this book, purchase a digital version to start reading immediately at the INTERSECTION Resource Page: intersection.zeroinfinancial.com.

Since the three books are not a prerequisite for using this devotional / journal, I'll recap the premise of the series here.

In several applications, there is a pivotal tool known as crosshairs. You find this point of reference in sharpshooting and surveying, for example. The operator's scope has two engraved lines to give a single place to focus when aiming at a target.

There is a reference for the horizontal plane and one for the vertical plane. The purpose is to align the crosshairs, where the two lines intersect, with the bullseye. Aiming to hit the bullseye requires precision and, using the simple principle of intersecting lines, you can easily pinpoint that target.

When peering through the scope of your financial future, there are several targets you should aim for. Before you focus on the bullseye, you must ensure the crosshairs are zeroed-in or correctly calibrated to guarantee hitting your target.

The area that you must focus on is where the two lines intersect. In our case, those two planes are God's Wealth and God's Wisdom. Once you have these two crosshairs in focus and zeroed-in, you can aim right at the center of your target and hit it consistently.

This book series is for anyone who wants to understand the foundational principles of money. Each book is genuinely a one-size-fits-all because it reveals foundational principles instead of custom strategies. It doesn't matter your current age, wage, or stage. These are vital truths for every individual's financial life.

As a financial coach, I sit down and help people, face to face, knee cap to knee cap, and when they need a hug, shoulder to shoulder. It may be online or in-person, but in either case, my job is to listen, teach, and help guide them through a personal, tailor-made plan.

This plan is *their* plan, unique to their situation, goals, and aspirations. Zero In Financial® has a mission to help every client, reader, customer, follower, and fan zero in.

We will walk with you as you
RECOVER from past money mistakes,
GROW your present pocketbook position, and
ZERO IN on your future financial fortune,
ultimately leaving a lasting legacy of love.

You need to RECOVER, GROW, and ZERO IN, but in your unique personal way. Although your resulting strategy is custom tailored, each must stay rooted in the same foundational principles found in the Word of God.

This book series will take you step by step through the foundational truths I use every day in coaching. Customization builds on top of these basic principles. Coaching is less about me talking and more about me actively listening. Everyone needs a mentor and coach, and I fill those voids as I encourage and guide. Even with the plethora of financial challenges you likely face, it comes down to the basics. When it's time to teach, this series is the playbook.

Again, if you want to pinpoint your financial destiny, you need to zero-in on your target, not someone else's mark. One of the most critical steps is knowing where you are aiming. I will walk you through discovering your target so you can zero-in with confidence.

You may have your financial target in sight but have yet to fix your focus. Have you ever heard the advice to fix your eyes on Jesus? That is expert advice and will surely do wonders for your financial plan. When you have the wrong perspective and have not fixed your financial plan according to God's Wisdom, you will miss the mark. You must manage God's Wealth with the proper point of view.

The blessings come where the two lines meet. So, it's time you have a focal point; let's reveal the perfect intersection of God's Wealth and God's Wisdom for your life.

PART I

Days 1 – 30

Welcome to Part 1 of 3. For the first 30 days, this guide will walk with you through INTERSECTION: *Biblical Faith Meet Financial Strategy — How to Lay a Solid Foundation for Prosperity.*

The scriptures teach us to be in a relationship with God, not religion. Your Heavenly Father wants you to live a prosperous life, and the Bible teaches you the proper way to handle that wealth. And the final twelve days of this part will show you how financial prosperity and the Fruit of the Spirit intersect.

Once you understand and begin living by these foundational truths, your heart will overflow with love, joy, and peace. Your actions will be purposeful with patience, kindness, and goodness. And your thoughts will be faithful and meek with self-control.

These are not only Christian financial concepts and principles; these are financial truths. It's time for you to RECOVER, GROW, and ZERO IN on your financial target.

_____

_____

_____

_____

_____

_____

_____

_____

_____

_____

_____

_____

_____

_____

_____

_____

_____

_____

Day 1

Reading:

- Introduction — Taking Aim
- Chapter 1 : Live in Christ Jesus — Living the Dream

Key Scripture:

To you who have received a faith as valuable as ours. You received that faith because our God and Savior Jesus Christ is fair and does what is right. Grace and peace be given to you more and more. You will have grace and peace because you truly know God and Jesus our Lord. Jesus has the power of God. His power has given us everything we need to live and to serve God. We have these things because we know him. Jesus called us by his glory and goodness. Through his glory and goodness, he gave us the very great and rich gifts he promised us. With those gifts you can share in God's nature (2 Peter 1:1-4 ICB).

Questions:

- What are the biggest dreams and aspirations you are aiming your financial life at?_____

_____

_____

_____

- Referring to your answer above, no matter how crystal clear it seems to you, how are you living your dream?_____

_____

_____

_____

Journal about ...

... your dream: Write it, Draw it.

... scars that prevent you from dreaming ...

... your prayer asking God to help you discover, live, and fulfill His purpose for your life ...

_____

_____

_____

_____

_____

_____

_____

_____

_____

_____

_____

_____

_____

_____

Day 2

Reading:

Chapter 1 : Live in Christ Jesus — Let Christ Be Lord and Savior

Key Scripture:

We believe that we are all saved the same way, by the undeserved grace of the Lord Jesus (Acts of the Apostles 15:11 NLT).

Questions:

- Have you asked Jesus to be Lord and Savior of your life?_____

  _____

  _____

  _____

- How does it feel to be sin debt free? And who are you going to share this great news with today?_____

  _____

  _____

  _____

- If you have not prayed to be saved, what is holding your back?_____

  _____

Download the free resource, "Life Development—A New Believer's Guide to Growing in Christ," here: salvation.zeroinfinancial.com

Journal about ...

    ... ways Jesus feels near and in what areas of your
    life God feels far away ...
    ... how you are going to nurture your faith ...

Day 3

Reading:

- Chapter 1 : Live in Christ Jesus — Let Christ Be Servant and King
- Chapter 1 : Live in Christ Jesus — Let Christ Be Master and Teacher

Key Scripture:

So when they had rowed about five and twenty or thirty furlongs, they see Jesus walking on the sea, and drawing nigh unto the ship: and they were afraid. But he saith unto them, It is I; be not afraid. Then they willingly received him into the ship: and immediately the ship was at the land whither they went (John 6:19-21).

Questions:

- What do you think about the fact that Jesus is both Servant and King?_____

_____

_____

_____

- In what ways can you grow in your learning from the Greatest Financial Teacher, God?

_____

_____

- What have you learned about reaching your life's destination by reading this passage?

Journal about …

... ways you can begin to be more like Jesus ...

... any apprehension about letting Jesus into your boat ...

... how you are going to allow the Master to be over everything in your life, including your finances ...

Day 4

Reading:

Chapter 2 : Not So Religious — Relationship Over Religion

Key Scripture:

But my God shall supply all your need according to his riches in glory by Christ Jesus (Philippians 4:19).

Questions:

- From your experience, how is relationship superior to religion?_____

  _____

  _____

  _____

- How does it feel to know that you have direct access to the Creator of everything, and He will supply all you need?_____

  _____

  _____

- Do you feel comfortable asking God for anything?_____

  _____

_____

_____

Journal about ...

... ways you can get closer and more intimate with
your Father ...

... scriptures you have found helpful when you
feel like your relationship with God is not the
best ...

... ways you best communicate with Christ and
hear the Holy Spirit speak to you ...

_____

_____

_____

_____

_____

_____

_____

_____

_____

_____

_____

_____

_____

Day 5

Reading:

- Chapter 2 : Not So Religious — Why the Bible

Key Scripture:

All scripture is given by inspiration of God, and is profitable for doctrine, for reproof, for correction, for instruction in righteousness (2 Timothy 3:16).

Questions:

- Are you surprised that there are over 2,000 verses in the Bible concerning every area of finances? Why or why not?_____

_____

_____

- What are your thoughts about the accuracy of your favorite version of the Holy Scriptures?

_____

_____

- Do you have at least a mustard seed of faith in the Word of God?_____

_____

_____

_____

_____

Journal about ...

... how you plan to read the Bible more often
and more consistently ...

... ways the Scripture gives you hope for your
specific financial situation in life ...

... doubts you have and need to confront ...

_____

_____

_____

_____

_____

_____

_____

_____

_____

_____

_____

_____

_____

_____

_____

_____

_____

_____

Day 6

Reading:

- Chapter 2 : Not So Religious — Listening to the Holy Spirit
- Chapter 2 : Not So Religious — Realizing Real Financial Freedom

Key Scripture:

However, as it is written: 'What no eye has seen, what no ear has heard, and what no human mind has conceived' — the things God has prepared for those who love him— these are the things God has revealed to us by his Spirit. The Spirit searches all things, even the deep things of God (1 Corinthians 2:9-10 NLT).

Questions:

- How is the Holy Spirit the source of true Financial Freedom?

  _____

  _____

  _____

- In what ways can you better live by the Spirit?

  _____

  _____

  _____

Download the free resource, "Financial Guidance from the Holy Spirit," here: intersection.zeroinfinancial.com

Journal about ...

... ways the Holy Spirit has been or you expect to be ...

- a Comforter in times of financial despair.
- an Intercessor when you have a list of needs.
- a Counselor when you need a career or money coach.
- a Source of Revelation when you just don't know what financial decision to make.
- an Agent of Reproof when you need correction.

_____

_____

_____

_____

_____

_____

_____

_____

_____

_____

_____

_____

_____

Day 7

Reading:

- Chapter 3 : You Need People — Intro
- Chapter 3 : You Need People — Why the Church is Imperfect but Vital

Key Scripture:

And let us consider one another to provoke unto love and to good works: Not forsaking the assembling of ourselves together, as the manner of some is; but exhorting one another: and so much the more, as ye see the day approaching (Hebrews 10:24-25).

Questions:

- Why is going to church in person at least once a week important for your financial health?_____

  _____

  _____

  _____

- How could you invest in your fellow Christian brothers and sisters?_____

  _____

  _____

  _____

- Have you found yourself taking for granted being with others at church in the past?

_____

_____

_____

_____

Journal about ...

... ways healthy Christian Fellowship will help you going forward ...

... people you know from church who you could begin building a stronger relationship with ...

_____

_____

_____

_____

_____

_____

_____

_____

_____

_____

_____

_____

Day 8

Reading:

- Chapter 3 : You Need People — You Need an Accountability Partner
- Chapter 3 : You Need People — Surround Yourself with Likeminded People

Key Scripture:

Confess your faults one to another, and pray one for another, that ye may be healed. The effectual fervent prayer of a righteous man availeth much (James 5:16).

Questions:

- What is the benefit of having an accountability partner?_____

_____

_____

_____

- How can your closest relationships have an effect on your financial focus?_____

_____

_____

_____

Journal about ...

... people who could be your accountability partner ...

... ways you can Prayerfully Plan (with your spouse if you are married) to maintain a healthy financial mindset ...

... the five closest people you have in your life ...

_____

_____

_____

_____

_____

_____

_____

_____

_____

_____

_____

_____

_____

_____

_____

_____

_____

_____

_____

Day 9

Reading:

Chapter 3 : You Need People — Relationships
Lead to Riches

Key Scripture:

Charge them that are rich in this world, that they be not
high-minded, nor trust in uncertain riches, but in the living
God, who giveth us richly all things to enjoy (1 Timothy
6:17).

Questions:

• How does comparing your own path to others
  position your potential prosperity?_____

  _____

  _____

  _____

• In what ways do relationships lead to riches?

  _____

  _____

  _____

  _____

*Download the free resource, "Financial Guidance from the Holy
Spirit," here: intersection.zeroinfinancial.com*

Journal about ...

... scriptures you will commit to memory that will help you continue to nurture your relationships ...

... making a plan to prune unhealthy relationships currently in your life ...

... things you hope to gain from your healthy relationships ...

_____

_____

_____

_____

_____

_____

_____

_____

_____

_____

_____

_____

_____

_____

_____

_____

_____

Day 10

Reading:

- Chapter 4 : Pray First — Intro
- Chapter 4 : Pray First — Resorting to Prayer

Key Scripture:

Don't worry about anything; instead, pray about everything. Tell God what you need and thank him for all he has done. Then you will experience God's peace, which exceeds anything we can understand. His peace will guard your hearts and minds as you live in Christ Jesus (Philippians 4:6-7 NLT).

Questions:

- Instead of being anxious, what aspects of your faith should you display?_____

_____

_____

_____

- What will be the effect on others when they see you calm in the midst of trying circumstances?

_____

_____

_____

_____

Journal about ...

... areas of your finances you tend to worry about ...

... how you are going to release all worries by giving them to God ...

... actions you can take the next time you are tempted to worry ...

_____

_____

_____

_____

_____

_____

_____

_____

_____

_____

_____

_____

_____

_____

_____

_____

_____

_____

_____

_____

Day 11

Reading:

Chapter 4 : Pray First — The Quick Fix

Key Scripture:

Pray without ceasing. In everything give thanks: for this is the will of God in Christ Jesus concerning you (1 Thessalonians 5:17-18).

Questions:

• What ways can a quick fix be worse than a more patient approach?_____

_____

_____

_____

_____

• Why is it important to pray for everything, small or large, at all times, continuously?_____

_____

_____

_____

_____

_____

Journal about ...

... a time when you prayed and had to wait but can be thankful looking back ...

... ways you can encourage someone who is praying and waiting in the midst of a financial dilemma ...

_____

_____

_____

_____

_____

_____

_____

_____

_____

_____

_____

_____

_____

_____

_____

_____

_____

_____

_____

_____

_____

Day 12

Reading:

- Chapter 4 : Pray First — Waiting
- Chapter 4 : Pray First — The Most Important Financial Target

Key Scripture:

But they that wait upon the Lord shall renew their strength; they shall mount up with wings as eagles; they shall run, and not be weary; and they shall walk, and not faint (Isaiah 40:31).

Questions:

- Why would someone be frustrated when they have been "waiting" but not "waiting upon the Lord"?_____

  _____

  _____

  _____

- Someone close to you has lost all strength and appears weary and faint; what do you tell them?

  _____

  _____

  _____

  _____

Journal about ...

... the characteristics of an eagle that make it
a perfect example of patience ...

... how you can grow your waiting muscle
when it comes to your financial goals and
dreams ...

Day 13

Reading:

- Chapter 5 : Don't Worry — Intro
- Chapter 5 : Don't Worry — Proper Planning

Key Scripture:

For the Scriptures tell us, "Abraham believed God, and God counted him as righteous because of his faith." When people work, their wages are not a gift, but something they have earned. But people are counted as righteous, not because of their work, but because of their faith in God who forgives sinners ... Clearly, God's promise to give the whole earth to Abraham and his descendants was based not on his obedience to God's law, but on a right relationship with God that comes by faith ... So the promise is received by faith. It is given as a free gift. And we are all certain to receive it, whether or not we live according to the law of Moses, if we have faith like Abraham's. For Abraham is the father of all who believe (Romans 4:3-5,13,16 NLT).

Questions:

- How does faith yield obedience and not vice versa?_____

_____

_____

_____

• Why must a powerful financial plan begin with prayer?

_____

_____

_____

Journal about ...

... what you can begin doing today to grow your faith ...

... God's promises for your future ...

_____

_____

_____

_____

_____

_____

_____

_____

_____

_____

_____

_____

_____

_____

Day 14

Reading:

Chapter 5 : Don't Worry — Proper Protection

Key Scripture:

When the storm is over ... good people, firm on their rock foundation, aren't even fazed (Proverbs 10:25 MSG).

Questions:

- How does God secure His wealth in your hands when you ask for His protection?_____

_____

_____

_____

_____

- Where in the Word of God does it say that it is wise to have advisors in your life?_____

_____

_____

_____

Journal about ...

... how faith in God has helped dissipate worry in your life...

… the areas of your finances which need better protection…

Day 15

Reading:

- Chapter 5 : Don't Worry — Proper Preparation
- Chapter 5 : Don't Worry — Proper Purpose & Position

Key Scripture:

Have them gather all the food produced in the good years that are just ahead and bring it to Pharaoh's storehouses. Store it away, and guard it so there will be food in the cities (Genesis 41:35 NLT).

Questions:

- Why does God allow there to be times of prosperity as well as times of famine?_____

_____

_____

_____

_____

- What are some reasons why God wants us to be financially prepared?_____

_____

_____

_____

Download the free resource, "Firm Foundation Life Development Study Guide," here: salvation.zeroinfinancial.com

Journal about ...

... how you can be better financially prepared ...

... what you need to do and when you are going to make those changes ...

... a prayer specific to God's promised purpose for your life ...

_____

_____

_____

_____

_____

_____

_____

_____

_____

_____

_____

_____

_____

_____

_____

_____

_____

_____

Day 16

Reading:

- Chapter 6 : Be Happy — Intro
- Chapter 6 : Be Happy — Contentment

Key Scripture:

But godliness with contentment is great gain. For we brought nothing into this world, and it is certain we can carry nothing out. And having food and raiment let us be therewith content (1 Timothy 6:6-8).

Questions:

- How does seeking the Kingdom of God first demonstrate our faith while working our strategy?_____

  _____

  _____

  _____

- How can contentment rooted in money be detrimental to happiness in life?_____

  _____

  _____

  _____

  _____

Journal about ...

    ... How you define happiness ...

    ... What contentment looks like in your life ...

Day 17

Reading:

Chapter 6 : Be Happy — Knowing What You Need

Key Scripture:

For what is a man advantaged, if he gain the whole world, and lose himself, or be cast away? (Luke 9:25)

Questions:

• How can we avoid getting ahead of God's plan for our lives?_____

_____

_____

_____

_____

• Why is it important to keep needs in proper perspective?_____

_____

_____

_____

_____

_____

Journal about ...

... The struggles you have when it comes it needs vs. wants ...

... A time when you bought something that you regretted and how it changed your purchasing decisions going forward ...

_____

_____

_____

_____

_____

_____

_____

_____

_____

_____

_____

_____

_____

_____

_____

_____

_____

_____

_____

_____

_____

Day 18

Reading:

- Chapter 6 : Be Happy — Opportunity Cost
- Chapter 6 : Be Happy — Financial Results
  Using a New Equation

Key Scripture:

Be very careful, then, how you live—not as unwise but as wise, making the most of every opportunity, because the days are evil. Therefore do not be foolish, but understand what the Lord's will is (Ephesians 5:15-17 NIV).

Questions:

- What is the definition of "opportunity cost"?___

  _____

  _____

  _____

  _____

- Since every decision is important, how can you be sure you have chosen wisely?_____

  _____

  _____

  _____

  _____

  _____

Journal about ...

... some ways you can think through purchasing
decisions with logic and strategy ...

... how you can lean on Godly relationships to
help keep opportunity cost in check ...

_____

_____

_____

_____

_____

_____

_____

_____

_____

_____

_____

_____

_____

_____

_____

_____

_____

_____

_____

_____

_____

_____

_____

_____

Day 19

Reading:

- Chapter 7 : Your Financial Vital Signs — Into
- Chapter 7 : Your Financial Vital Signs — What Drives You?

Key Scripture:

For the love of money is the root of all evil: which while some coveted after, they have erred from the faith, and pierced themselves through with many sorrows (1 Timothy 6:10).

Questions:

- Why is it important to keep tabs on your financial vital signs?_____

  _____

  _____

  _____

- What parallels do you see between physical fitness and fiscal fitness?_____

  _____

  _____

  _____

Journal about ...

> ... ways you are striving to be more financially healthy ...
>
> ... what drives you ...

_____

_____

_____

_____

_____

_____

_____

_____

_____

_____

_____

_____

_____

_____

_____

_____

_____

_____

_____

_____

_____

_____

Day 20

Reading:

Chapter 7 : Your Financial Vital Signs —
Checking Your Pulse

Key Scripture:

If therefore ye have not been faithful in the unrighteous mammon, who will commit to your trust the true riches? And if ye have not been faithful in that which is another man's, who shall give you that which is your own? No servant can serve two masters: for either he will hate the one, and love the other; or else he will hold to the one, and despise the other. Ye cannot serve God and mammon (Luke 16:11-13).

Questions:

- What is the definition of "mammon"?_____

  _____

  _____

  _____

- Why does the Bible warn us about improper uses of money?_____

  _____

  _____

  _____

Journal about ...

... Ways you are using money that you know are not right (Confess and release) ...

... Any hint of your financial pulse being abnormal ...

_____

_____

_____

_____

_____

_____

_____

_____

_____

_____

_____

_____

_____

_____

_____

_____

_____

_____

_____

_____

_____

_____

Day 21

Reading:

- Chapter 7 : Your Financial Vital Signs — Taking Your Temperature
- Chapter 7 : Your Financial Vital Signs — Your Financial Heart, Hands + Feet, and Head

Key Scripture:

Better is the poor that walketh in his uprightness, than he that is perverse in his ways, though he be rich (Proverbs 28:6).

Questions:

- What is the cure for an abnormal financial temperature?_____

_____

_____

_____

_____

- Why did Jesus tell the first church to wait on the Holy Spirit?_____

_____

_____

_____

_____

*Download the free resource, "Finances by the Fruit of the Spirit,"
here: intersection.zeroinfinancial.com*

Journal about ...

... How you feel about financial integrity ...

... Ways you can increasingly incorporate the Holy Spirit in your daily prayer ...

_____

_____

_____

_____

_____

_____

_____

_____

_____

_____

_____

_____

_____

_____

_____

_____

_____

_____

_____

Day 22

Reading:

- Chapter 8 : Your Financial Heart — Intro
- Chapter 8 : Your Financial Heart — Love

Key Scripture:

For where your treasure is, there will your heart be also (Matthew 6:21).

Questions:

- How does one's financial heart drive financial strategy?_____

_____

_____

_____

_____

_____

_____

- Who does Jesus instruct us to love?_____

_____

_____

_____

_____

_____

Journal about ...

... A time you have witnessed someone being financially generous and loving towards another ...

... Ways God has demonstrated financial love in your life ...

Day 23

Reading:

Chapter 8 : Your Financial Heart — Joy

Key Scripture:

Thou wilt shew me the path of life: in thy presence is fulness of joy; at thy right hand there are pleasures for evermore (Psalm 16:11).

Questions:

• How is your joy affected by your financial priorities?_____

_____

_____

_____

_____

• In what ways is heavenly joy greater than earthly happiness?_____

_____

_____

_____

_____

Journal about ...

... A recent experience full of financial joy ...

... Someone you need to pray for who has money but no true joy ...

_____

_____

_____

_____

_____

_____

_____

_____

_____

_____

_____

_____

_____

_____

_____

_____

_____

_____

_____

_____

_____

Day 24

Reading:

Chapter 8 : Your Financial Heart — Peace

Key Scripture:

And the peace of God, which passeth all understanding, shall keep your hearts and minds through Christ Jesus (Philippians 4:7).

Questions:

• Why is it essential for one's financial heart to be at peace?_____

_____

_____

_____

_____

• How can your thinking affect your financial heart's peace?_____

_____

_____

_____

_____

_____

Journal about ...

... Areas where your financial heart struggles ...
... Words you would use to describe peace ...

_____

_____

_____

_____

_____

_____

_____

_____

_____

_____

_____

_____

_____

_____

_____

_____

_____

_____

_____

_____

_____

_____

_____

Day 25

Reading:

- Chapter 9 : Your Financial Hands & Feet — Intro
- Chapter 9 : Your Financial Hands & Feet — Patience (Longsuffering)

Key Scripture:

But if we hope for that we see not, then do we with patience wait for it (Romans 8:25).

Questions:

- How does patience affect your financial hands and feet? _____

  _____

  _____

  _____

  _____

- Why does patience plus prayer produce perfect prosperity? _____

  _____

  _____

  _____

  _____

Download the free resource, "Finances by the Fruit of the Spirit,"
here: intersection.zeroinfinancial.com

Journal about ...

... A time patience would have saved you from a
financial blunder ...

... Emotions you have that are the archenemy of
patience ...

_____

_____

_____

_____

_____

_____

_____

_____

_____

_____

_____

_____

_____

_____

_____

Day 26

Reading:

Chapter 9 : Your Financial Hands & Feet — Kindness

Key Scripture:

And be ye kind one to another, tenderhearted, forgiving one another, even as God for Christ's sake hath forgiven you (Ephesians 4:32).

Questions:

• In what ways could someone be financially unkind?_____

_____

_____

_____

_____

• What is the reward for being kind?_____

_____

_____

_____

_____

_____

Journal about ...

... How you intend to be more kind ...

... Ways you can teach the children in your life about kindness ...

_____

_____

_____

_____

_____

_____

_____

_____

_____

_____

_____

_____

_____

_____

_____

_____

_____

_____

_____

_____

_____

Day 27

Reading:

Chapter 9 : Your Financial Hands & Feet — Goodness

Key Scripture:

And let us not be weary in well doing: for in due season we shall reap if we faint not. As we have therefore opportunity, let us do good unto all men, especially unto them who are of the household of faith (Galatians 6:9-10).

Questions:

• How can a financial plan be "morally excellent"?

_____

_____

_____

_____

_____

_____

• Why should we be good?_____

_____

_____

_____

_____

_____

Journal about ...

... Areas in which you can improve the function of your financial hands and feet...

... What goodness looks like in your family...

... how goodness shows through all your financial dealings ...

_____

_____

_____

_____

_____

_____

_____

_____

_____

_____

_____

_____

_____

_____

_____

_____

_____

_____

_____

_____

Day 28

Reading:

- Chapter 10 : Your Financial Head — Intro
- Chapter 10 : Your Financial Head — Faithfulness

Key Scripture:

He that is faithful in that which is least is faithful also in much: and he that is unjust in the least is unjust also in much. And if ye have not been faithful in that which is another man's, who shall give you that which is your own? (Luke 16:10,12)

Questions:

- What is the difference between being "carnally minded" and "spiritually minded"?_____

_____

_____

_____

- Why is faithfulness so attractive?_____

_____

_____

_____

Download the free resource, "Finances by the Fruit of the Spirit,"
here: intersection.zeroinfinancial.com

Journal about ...

... Ways you can be more faithful in your work ...

... How you will be applying faith to you financial strategy ...

_____

_____

_____

_____

_____

_____

_____

_____

_____

_____

_____

_____

_____

_____

_____

_____

_____

_____

_____

Day 29

Reading:

Chapter 10 : Your Financial Head — Gentleness
(Meekness)

Key Scripture:

By humility and the fear of the Lord are riches, and
honour, and life (Proverbs 22:4).

Questions:

• What is the definition of humility?_____

_____

_____

_____

_____

_____

• What does the Bible mean by the phrase "fear of
the Lord"?_____

_____

_____

_____

_____

_____

Journal about ...

... what you have learned from Moses' life ...

... how your future wealth will affect your meekness ...

_____

_____

_____

_____

_____

_____

_____

_____

_____

_____

_____

_____

_____

_____

_____

_____

_____

_____

_____

_____

_____

Day 30

Reading:

- Chapter 10 : Your Financial Head — Self-Control (Temperance)
- Conclusion — Freedom at the Intersection

Key Scripture:

A person without self-control is like a city with broken-down walls (Proverbs 25:28 NLT).

Questions:

- How does self-control effect your financial mindset?_____

  _____

  _____

  _____

  _____

  _____

- In what ways can one be financially incontinent?

  _____

  _____

  _____

  _____

Download the free resource, "Firm Foundation Life Development Study Guide," here: salvation.zeroinfinancial.com

Journal about ...

... Struggles you may realize between your relationship with money and your relationship with God ...

... Attributes of your financial heart or hands & feet that would function improperly if lacking self-control ...

_____

_____

_____

_____

_____

_____

_____

_____

_____

_____

_____

_____

_____

_____

_____

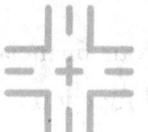

PART II

Days 31 – 60

Welcome to Part 2 of 3. For the next 30 days, this guide will walk with you through INTERSECTION: *God's Ownership Meets Money Management — How to Be a Good and Faithful Steward.*

Our God is an amazing Creator and an awesome Owner of everything in heaven and on earth. Genesis gives an account of where wealth comes from, who gets to handle it all, and how it should be managed. It would be best to manage God's Wealth with God's Wisdom, and this part will show you the spiritual and practical laws to follow.

There may be no other guide that goes into so much detail about the tithe, for we will spend nine days going deep into the subject. Yes, ten percent of the 90 days will be spent reading, praying, learning, and applying the truths of tithing.

The final chapter of this book and the last three days of this part will explore how to manage money according to The Ten Commandments with New Testament application. Once you understand and begin living by these foundational truths, you won't be tempted by the false god of mammon, and you will be able to avoid all prosperity limiting thoughts. Instead, you will get proper renewal and have a sharp money mindset to carry out God's work with excellence, managing His money with love and joy.

These are not only Christian financial concepts and principles; these are financial truths. It's time for you to RECOVER, GROW, and ZERO IN on your financial target.

Day 31

Reading:

- Introduction — Fixing Your Focus
- Chapter 1 : The Creation — Intro

Key Scripture:

In the beginning God created the heaven and the earth"
(Genesis 1:1).

Questions:

- How does a relationship with Jesus save your soul, keep you balanced, and help you stay healthy in life's many facets, including money?___

_____

_____

_____

_____

_____

- Name some of the many roles God plays in your life:_____

_____

_____

_____

_____

Journal about ...

... Your doubts about God being the Creator of everything ...

... The things God is leading you to focus on ...

_____

_____

_____

_____

_____

_____

_____

_____

_____

_____

_____

_____

_____

_____

_____

_____

_____

_____

_____

_____

_____

_____

Day 32

Reading:

- Chapter 1 : The Creation — He Created the Heavens
- Chapter 1 : The Creation — He Created the Earth

Key Scripture:

Praise ye the Lord. Praise ye the Lord from the heavens: praise him in the heights. Praise him, ye heavens of heavens, and ye waters that be above the heavens. Let them praise the name of the Lord: for he commanded, and they were created (Psalm 148:1,4-5).

Questions:

- Why is intentional order important when creating? _____

_____

_____

_____

- How do managers show loyalty to the owner?

_____

_____

_____

_____

Journal about ...

... Any desires you have to create, design, write, invent, ...

... Theories your learned in school concerning the origin of earth and space ...

Day 33

Reading:

- Chapter 1 : The Creation — He Created the Cattle and the Hills
- Chapter 1 : The Creation — He Created You and Me

Key Scripture:

And God blessed them, and God said unto them, Be fruitful, and multiply, and replenish the earth, and subdue it: and have dominion over the fish of the sea, and over the fowl of the air, and over every living thing that moveth upon the earth. And God said, Behold, I have given you every herb bearing seed, which is upon the face of all the earth, and every tree, in the which is the fruit of a tree yielding seed; to you it shall be for meat. And to every beast of the earth, and to every fowl of the air, and to every thing that creepeth upon the earth, wherein there is life, I have given every green herb for meat: and it was so (Genesis 1:28-30).

Questions:

- How can you plan for the wealth you've been tasked to manage to compound and multiply?___

_____

_____

• What are the first four tasks God gave Adam and
Eve?_____

_____

_____

_____

Journal about ...

... What life could look like with no violence, no
death, no struggle ...

... A time when God needed to have "the talk"
with you ...

_____

_____

_____

_____

_____

_____

_____

_____

_____

_____

_____

Day 34

Reading:

Chapter 2 : The Law — Intro

Key Scripture:

… **if thou shalt hearken diligently unto the voice of the LORD thy God, to observe and to do all his commandments … all these blessings shall come on thee, and overtake thee,** … Blessed shalt thou be in the city, and blessed shalt thou be in the field. Blessed shall be the fruit of thy body, and the fruit of thy ground, and the fruit of thy cattle, the increase of thy kine, and the flocks of thy sheep. Blessed shall be thy basket and thy store. Blessed shalt thou be when thou comest in, and blessed shalt thou be when thou goest out. … **But it shall come to pass, if thou wilt not hearken unto the voice of the LORD thy God, to observe to do all his commandments and his statutes which I command thee this day; that all these curses shall come upon thee, and overtake thee:** cursed shalt thou be in the city, and cursed shalt thou be in the field. Cursed shall be thy basket and thy store. Cursed shall be the fruit of thy body, and the fruit of thy land, the increase of thy kine, and the flocks of thy sheep. Cursed shalt thou be when thou comest in, and cursed shalt thou be when thou goest out … (Deuteronomy 28:2-6,15-19).

Questions:

- Obedience leads to _____.
- _____ leads to Condemnation.
- What actions accompany respect for authority?

_____

_____

_____

Journal about ...

... ways you have seen children disrespect
authority ...

... different things God has clearly told you to do ...

_____

_____

_____

_____

_____

_____

_____

_____

_____

_____

_____

_____

_____

_____

_____

Day 35

Reading:

- Chapter 2 : The Law — The Owner Gets to Make the Rules
- Chapter 2 : The Law — Healthy Boundaries

Key Scripture:

This book of the law shall not depart out of thy mouth; but thou shalt meditate therein day and night, that thou mayest observe to do according to all that is written therein: for then thou shalt make thy way prosperous, and then thou shalt have good success (Joshua 1:8).

Questions:

- How can we ensure our prosperity and success?

  _____

  _____

  _____

  _____

- What was the result of Adam and Eve's disobedience?_____

  _____

  _____

  _____

  _____

Journal about ...

... How rules keep your relationship with authority healthy ...

... A time when you were in authority and put boundaries in place ...

_____

_____

_____

_____

_____

_____

_____

_____

_____

_____

_____

_____

_____

_____

_____

_____

_____

_____

_____

_____

Day 36

Reading:

Chapter 2 : The Law — God's Wisdom Leads to
the Good Life

Key Scripture:

Think not that I am come to destroy the law, or the
prophets: I am not come to destroy, but to fulfil. For verily
I say unto you, Till heaven and earth pass, one jot or one
tittle shall in no wise pass from the law, till all be fulfilled
(Matthew 5:17-18).

Questions:

• What is the purpose of the law?_____

_____

_____

_____

_____

• Why is it best to aim for where God's wisdom—
which He shows us in His law—intersects with
God's wealth—which He freely gives us?_____

_____

_____

_____

_____

Download the free resource, "Life Development—A New Believer's Guide to Growing in Christ," here: salvation.zeroinfinancial.com

Journal about ...

... Ways you have found liberty through rules and regulations ...

... Your personal definition of the "good life" ...

Day 37

Reading:

- Chapter 3 : The Redemption — Intro
- Chapter 3 : The Redemption — God Gave His
  Creation Free Will

Key Scripture:

But a certain man named Ananias, with Sapphira his wife, sold a possession, And kept back part of the price, his wife also being privy to it, and brought a certain part, and laid it at the apostles' feet. But Peter said, Ananias, why hath Satan filled thine heart to lie to the Holy Ghost, and to keep back part of the price of the land? Whiles it remained, was it not thine own? and after it was sold, was it not in thine own power? why hast thou conceived this thing in thine heart? thou hast not lied unto men, but unto God. And Ananias hearing these words fell down, and gave up the ghost: and great fear came on all them that heard these things (Acts 5:1-5).

Questions:

- What are some of the "traps" people fall into when trying to get ahead with money?_____

  _____

  _____

_____

_____

• How does lying and cheating affect our financial outcome?_____

_____

_____

_____

Journal about ...

   ... Ways you can manage God's wealth by His example of patience and forgiveness ...

   ... Decisions you have made that have led to prosperity or hardship ...

_____

_____

_____

_____

_____

_____

_____

_____

_____

_____

_____

_____

Day 38

Reading:

- Chapter 3 : The Redemption — God Has the Right to Judge His Creation
- Chapter 3 : The Redemption — God Made a Way for His Creation

Key Scripture:

I have discovered this principle of life—that when I want to do what is right, I inevitably do what is wrong. I love God's law with all my heart. But there is another power within me that is at war with my mind. This power makes me a slave to the sin that is still within me. Oh, what a miserable person I am! Who will free me from this life that is dominated by sin and death? Thank God! The answer is in Jesus Christ our Lord. So you see how it is: In my mind I really want to obey God's law, but because of my sinful nature I am a slave to sin (Romans 7:21-25 NLT).

Questions:

- Why do bad things happen in the world?_____

_____

_____

_____

_____

• In what ways do we resemble God the Creator?

_____

_____

_____

• What is the result when Jesus and the law intersect?_____

_____

_____

_____

Journal about ...

... Ways you can encourage someone who had incurred loss ...

... Differences you see between the world's way and God's way of managing money ...

_____

_____

_____

_____

_____

_____

_____

_____

_____

_____

_____

Day 39

Reading:

Chapter 3 : The Redemption — God is in Control

Key Scripture:

And the Lord, he it is that doth go before thee; he will be with thee, he will not fail thee, neither forsake thee: fear not, neither be dismayed (Deuteronomy 31:8).

Questions:

• What is your financial vehicle's destination when Jesus is at the wheel?_____

_____

_____

_____

• How can you pattern your life after the widow who served Elijah?_____

_____

_____

_____

Journal about ...

... Provisions you are trusting the Lord for ...

... Ways you can let go and let God ...

Day 40

Reading:

- Chapter 4 : What Tithing Is and Is Not — Intro
- Chapter 4 : What Tithing Is and Is Not — Not Giving

Key Scripture:

And the Lord God commanded the man, saying, Of every tree of the garden thou mayest freely eat: But of the tree of the knowledge of good and evil, thou shalt not eat of it: for in the day that thou eatest thereof thou shalt surely die (Genesis 2:16-17).

Questions:

- Why do boundaries exist in all healthy owner-manager relationships?_____

  _____

  _____

  _____

  _____

- What is the difference between offerings and tithes?_____

  _____

  _____

  _____

Journal about ...

... Your thoughts concerning God having a
portion that ought not be touched ...

... Ways you could teach a young child the
principle of tithing by using the story of Adam
and Eve ...

_____

_____

_____

_____

_____

_____

_____

_____

_____

_____

_____

_____

_____

_____

_____

_____

_____

_____

_____

_____

Day 41

Reading:

- Chapter 4 : What Tithing Is and Is Not — First and Best
- Chapter 4 : What Tithing Is and Is Not — Ten Percent

Key Scripture:

You will be accepted if you do what is right. But if you refuse to do what is right, then watch out!" (Genesis 4:7a NLT)

Questions:

- What did Cain do wrong when he presented his offering before God?_____

  _____

  _____

  _____

  _____

- Why do some people get tithing mixed up with amounts other than ten percent?_____

  _____

  _____

  _____

  _____

Journal about ...

... Your financial history when it comes to tithing ...

... How you will incorporate tithing into your financial plan ...

_____

_____

_____

_____

_____

_____

_____

_____

_____

_____

_____

_____

_____

_____

_____

_____

_____

_____

_____

_____

_____

_____

_____

_____

Day 42

Reading:

Chapter 4 : What Tithing Is and Is Not — Pursue Truth

Key Scripture:

...if ye continue in my word, then are ye my disciples indeed; And ye shall know the truth, and **the truth shall make you free** (John 8:31-32).

Questions:

- Why is there always opposition towards the truth?_____

  _____

  _____

  _____

  _____

- In what ways do all laws (physical, financial, spiritual ...) continue to operate as intended no matter what choices you make?_____

  _____

  _____

  _____

  _____

  _____

Journal about ...

... Any mental battles you have about tithing ...

... changes you need to make in your money management ...

Day 43

Reading:

- Chapter 5 : Protection & Prosperity — Intro
- Chapter 5 : Protection & Prosperity — The Most Significant Foundation Stone

Key Scripture:

And this memorial pillar I have set up will become a place for worshiping God, and I will present to God a tenth of everything he gives me (Genesis 28:22 NLT).

Questions:

- Why do we all seek prosperity and protection?___

  _____

  _____

  _____

  _____

  _____

- Why is tithing the most significant decision you can make with money?_____

  _____

  _____

  _____

  _____

Journal about ...

... Ways you can make sure you pass down
generational wisdom concerning tithing ...

... How Biblical tithing will shape your prayers
concerning finances ...

_____

_____

_____

_____

_____

_____

_____

_____

_____

_____

_____

_____

_____

_____

_____

_____

_____

_____

_____

_____

_____

Day 44

Reading:

- Chapter 5 : Protection & Prosperity — The First Line of Defense

Key Scripture:

And I will rebuke the devourer for your sakes, and he shall not destroy the fruits of your ground; neither shall your vine cast her fruit before the time in the field, saith the Lord of hosts (Malachi 3:11).

Questions:

- What are some of the benefits of tithing?_____

_____

_____

_____

_____

- How do these verses in Malachi relate to the stories in Genesis?_____

_____

_____

_____

_____

Journal about ...

 ... Your thoughts about the existence of a
  devourer ...

 ... How you will secure your financial plan ...

_____

_____

_____

_____

_____

_____

_____

_____

_____

_____

_____

_____

_____

_____

_____

_____

_____

_____

_____

_____

_____

_____

Day 45

Reading:

Chapter 5 : Protection & Prosperity — God Promises Prosperity

Key Scripture:

"Bring all the tithes into the storehouse so there will be enough food in my Temple. If you do," says the Lord of Heaven's Armies, "I will open the windows of heaven for you. I will pour out a blessing so great you won't have enough room to take it in! Try it! Put me to the test!" (Malachi 3:10 NLT)

Questions:

• Where is the proper place to return the tithe? Why?_____

_____

_____

_____

• What is the benefit of tithing by check or cash as opposed to online?_____

_____

_____

_____

_____

Make sure to check out the INTERSECTION Resource Page for more wisdom about tithing and all other subjects in this book series here: intersection.zeroinfinancial.com.

Journal about ...

... How you feel about putting God to the test ...

... Your thoughts around not having to experience adverse situations because they were blocked by divine providence before ever reaching you ...

_____

_____

_____

_____

_____

_____

_____

_____

_____

_____

_____

_____

_____

_____

_____

_____

Day 46

Reading:

- Chapter 6 : God's Examples — Intro
- Chapter 6 : God's Examples — Scripture Meets Nature

Key Scripture:

Blessed is the man that walketh not in the counsel of the ungodly, nor standeth in the way of sinners, nor sitteth in the seat of the scornful. But his delight is in the law of the Lord ; and in his law doth he meditate day and night. And he shall be like a tree planted by the rivers of water, that bringeth forth his fruit in his season; his leaf also shall not wither; and whatsoever he doeth shall prosper (Psalm 1:1-3).

Questions:

- What have been the ramifications of the lack of tithing amongst Christians in America?_____

  _____

  _____

- Where is "tithing" mentioned for the first time in the Bible?_____

  _____

_____

_____

Journal about ...

... How your thoughts around tithing have changed over the last few days ...

... Observing the tithe in manifested nature ...

_____

_____

_____

_____

_____

_____

_____

_____

_____

_____

_____

_____

_____

_____

_____

_____

_____

_____

Day 47

Reading:

Chapter 6 : God's Examples — Jesus Reinforced
the Tithe

Key Scripture:

What sorrow awaits you teachers of religious law and you
Pharisees. Hypocrites! For you are careful to tithe even the
tiniest income from your herb gardens, but you ignore the
more important aspects of the law—justice, mercy, and
faith. **You should tithe, yes,** but do not neglect the more
important things (Matthew 23:23 NLT).

Questions:

• How do Jesus' words to the Pharisees reinforce
relationship over religion?_____

_____

_____

_____

_____

• In what ways can tithing become legalistic?_____

_____

_____

_____

_____

Journal about ...

... The similarities between not returning the tithe
and not paying honest taxes ...

... How tithing out of love makes you feel ...

_____

_____

_____

_____

_____

_____

_____

_____

_____

_____

_____

_____

_____

_____

_____

_____

_____

_____

_____

_____

_____

_____

Day 48

Reading:

Chapter 6 : God's Examples — God Beat Us to the Punch

Key Scripture:

For God so loved the world, that he gave his only begotten Son, that whosoever believeth in him should not perish, but have everlasting life (John 3:16).

Questions:

• What did God get in return for His tithe, Jesus?

_____

_____

_____

_____

• How should God's example shape our posture in tithing?_____

_____

_____

_____

_____

_____

Journal about ...

... How God giving His First and Best makes you feel ...

... The changes in your financial plan you are going to make today ...

_____

_____

_____

_____

_____

_____

_____

_____

_____

_____

_____

_____

_____

_____

_____

_____

_____

_____

_____

_____

_____

_____

Day 49

Reading:

- Chapter 7 : Working — Intro
- Chapter 7 : Working — Work Is Not a Curse

Key Scripture:

And the Lord God planted a garden eastward in Eden; and there he put the man whom he had formed. And the Lord God took the man, and put him into the garden of Eden **to dress it and to keep it** (Genesis 2:8,15).

Questions:

- Why is rest important for work?_____

_____

_____

_____

_____

- In what ways can you make work as enjoyable as possible?_____

_____

_____

_____

_____

Journal about ...

... Ways you need to begin consulting God in your financial plan ...

... How you can begin applying His prescription towards your God-given purpose with your portion ...

_____

_____

_____

_____

_____

_____

_____

_____

_____

_____

_____

_____

_____

_____

_____

_____

_____

_____

_____

_____

_____

_____

Day 50

Reading:

Chapter 7 : Working — It's Tough But Good For
You

Key Scripture:

Be ye strong therefore, and let not your hands be weak: for
your work shall be rewarded (2 Chronicles 15:7).

Questions:

• What is the reward for working?_____

_____

_____

_____

_____

_____

• How can you resist the temptation to not work
hard?_____

_____

_____

_____

_____

_____

Journal about ...

... Ways you can dedicate your work to the Lord ...

... What God is doing through you in your current job ...

Day 51

Reading:

- Chapter 7 : Working — Laziness is Not a Gift
- Chapter 7 : Working — Position In Your Purpose

Key Scripture:

And we know that all things work together for good to them that love God, to them who are the called according to his purpose (Romans 8:28).

Questions:

- How can you combat the biggest enemy of work?_____

  _____

  _____

  _____

- What is the process of positioning your career towards God's purpose?_____

  _____

  _____

  _____

  _____

Journal about ...

   ... Ways you can help someone who feels as if they are disadvantaged ...

   ... Your purpose; What you feel God leading you to do ...

Day 52

Reading:

- Chapter 8 : Learning — Intro
- Chapter 8 : Learning — Financial Degree from Proverbs

Key Scripture:

Also, that the soul be without knowledge, it is not good; and he that hasteth with his feet sinneth (Proverbs 19:2).

Questions:

- What are three ways you can increase your financial IQ?_____

  _____

  _____

  _____

  _____

- In your life, what non tangible things have higher value than financial riches?_____

  _____

  _____

  _____

  _____

Journal about ...

... Ways you can apply the book of Proverbs to your daily financial life ...

... The way your relationship with God and others is connected to money management according to Proverbs ...

_____

_____

_____

_____

_____

_____

_____

_____

_____

_____

_____

_____

_____

_____

_____

_____

_____

_____

_____

_____

_____

Day 53

Reading:

Chapter 8 : Learning — Higher Education is
Overrated

Key Scripture:

All Scripture is God-breathed and is useful for teaching,
rebuking, correcting and training in righteousness
(2 Timothy 3:16 NIV).

Questions:

• It what ways is our system of education overrated?

_____

_____

_____

• How has using the Bible for teaching been
underutilized?_____

_____

_____

_____

• What alternatives are there to going to college
directly after high school?_____

_____

_____

_____

Journal about ...

... How higher education has played a role in your life ...

... Ways you can encourage others in your life to not fall for the mainstream messaging that surrounds university life ...

_____

_____

_____

_____

_____

_____

_____

_____

_____

_____

_____

_____

_____

_____

_____

_____

_____

Day 54

Reading:

> Chapter 8 : Learning — Where Wisdom Meets
> Real Education

Key Scripture:

My son, if thou wilt receive my words, and hide my
commandments with thee; So that thou incline thine ear
unto wisdom, and apply thine heart to understanding; Yea,
if thou criest after knowledge, and liftest up thy voice for
understanding; If thou seekest her as silver, and searchest
for her as for hid treasures; Then shalt thou understand the
fear of the Lord, and find the knowledge of God. For the
Lord giveth wisdom: out of his mouth cometh knowledge
and understanding (Proverbs 2:1-6).

Questions:

- Why should you not rely on government schools
  alone to teach your child?_____

  _____

  _____

  _____

- What are some reasons there is a lack of financial
  education in the home today?_____

  _____

Journal about ...

... Ways you can guide the young people in your life ...

... Alternatives to textbooks, Wikipedia, and other mainstream learning resources ...

Day 55

Reading:

- Chapter 9 : Managing — Intro
- Chapter 9 : Managing — Manage the Garden

Key Scripture:

After this manner therefore pray ye: Our Father which art in heaven, Hallowed be thy name. Thy kingdom come. Thy will be done in earth, as it is in heaven. Give us this day our daily bread. And forgive us our debts, as we forgive our debtors. And lead us not into temptation, but deliver us from evil: For thine is the kingdom, and the power, and the glory, for ever. Amen (Matthew 6:9-13).

Questions:

- In what ways could obedience be poorly executed?_____

_____

_____

_____

- Why is budgeting essential for managing money with excellence?_____

_____

_____

_____

Download the God's Ownership Meets Money Management SWOT Analysis worksheet on the INTERSECTION Resource page: intersection.zeroinfinancial.com.

Journal about ...

... How you will apply the Lord's prayer in future situations ...

... Your strengths, your weaknesses, your opportunities, your threats ...

_____

_____

_____

_____

_____

_____

_____

_____

_____

_____

_____

_____

_____

_____

_____

_____

_____

_____

Day 56

Reading:

Chapter 9 : Managing — Investing What You
Manage

Key Scripture:

The wise have wealth and luxury, but fools spend whatever
they get (Proverbs 21:20).

Questions:

• Why is investing important?_____

_____

_____

_____

_____

_____

_____

• What is a sinking fund?_____

_____

_____

_____

_____

_____

_____

Journal about ...

... How you have viewed investing in the past and how you will begin to incorporate it into your plan ...

... Items and events you could start a sinking fund for today ...

_____

_____

_____

_____

_____

_____

_____

_____

_____

_____

_____

_____

_____

_____

_____

_____

_____

_____

_____

_____

_____

Day 57

Reading:

Chapter 9 : Managing — Entrepreneurship is
Biblical

Key Scripture:

She makes sure her dealings are profitable; her lamp burns
late into the night (Proverbs 31:18 NLT).

Questions:

• How were entrepreneurs used in the Bible to
demonstrate the gospel message?_____

_____

_____

_____

_____

• What are some reasons someone might be
apprehensive in starting a business?_____

_____

_____

_____

_____

_____

Journal about ...

... Your dream venture ...

... Any entrepreneurs in your life you could pray for and/or support ...

_____

_____

_____

_____

_____

_____

_____

_____

_____

_____

_____

_____

_____

_____

_____

_____

_____

_____

_____

_____

_____

Day 58

Reading:

- Chapter 10 : Money Management by The Ten Commandments — Intro

- Chapter 10 : Money Management by The Ten Commandments — THOU SHALT HAVE NO OTHER GODS BEFORE ME

- Chapter 10 : Money Management by The Ten Commandments — THOU SHALT NOT MAKE UNTO THEE ANY GRAVEN IMAGE

- Chapter 10 : Money Management by The Ten Commandments — THOU SHALT NOT TAKE THE NAME OF THE LORD THY GOD IN VAIN

- Chapter 10 : Money Management by The Ten Commandments — REMEMBER THE SABBATH DAY, TO KEEP IT HOLY

Key Scripture:

After this manner therefore pray ye: Our Father which art in heaven, Hallowed be thy name (Matthew 6:9).

Questions:

- How do you feel about The Ten Commandments being taken out of the court room and the classroom as it once was?_____

_____

_____

_____

- In what ways have people replaced God in their lives with monetary and material things?_____

_____

_____

_____

- What has been the result of society forsaking the sabbath?_____

_____

_____

_____

Journal about ...

... A _checkup from the neck-up_ surrounding your spiritual and financial priorities ...

... Ways you can protect your sabbath ...

_____

_____

_____

_____

_____

_____

_____

_____

Day 59

Reading:

- Chapter 10 : Money Management by The Ten Commandments — HONOUR THY FATHER AND THY MOTHER
- Chapter 10 : Money Management by The Ten Commandments — THOU SHALT NOT KILL
- Chapter 10 : Money Management by The Ten Commandments — THOU SHALT NOT COMMIT ADULTERY

Key Scripture:

But the fearful, and unbelieving, and the abominable, and murderers, and whoremongers, and sorcerers, and idolaters, and all liars, shall have their part in the lake which burneth with fire and brimstone: which is the second death (Revelation 21:8).

Questions:

- In what ways has a respect for authority been instilled in your family?_____

_____

_____

- What are some of the most common regrets of someone on their deathbed?_____

_____

_____

_____

- Hating others leads to _____ ;
  _____ others leads to liberty.

Journal about ...

... How you can make forgiving others a natural
response ...

... Confessing any financial infidelity in your life ...

_____

_____

_____

_____

_____

_____

_____

_____

_____

_____

_____

_____

_____

_____

_____

_____

_____

_____

Day 60

Reading:

- Chapter 10 : Money Management by The Ten Commandments — THOU SHALT NOT STEAL
- Chapter 10 : Money Management by The Ten Commandments — THOU SHALT NOT BEAR FALSE WITNESS
- Chapter 10 : Money Management by The Ten Commandments — THOU SHALT NOT COVET
- Conclusion — The Greatest Commandments

Key Scripture:

Have nothing to do with "…fornication, uncleanness, inordinate affection, evil concupiscence, and covetousness, which is idolatry" (Colossians 3:5).

Questions:

- How do people justify "white lies" or stealing things that are of small value?_____

_____

_____

_____

- What is the definition of covetousness?_____

_____

Download the Poster, Money Management by the Ten Commandments, on the INTERSECTION Resource page here: intersection.zeroinfinancial.com.

Journal about ...

... Ways you can teach the young people in your life about all the commandments ...

... Any tinge of theft, false words, or covetousness in your life ...

... Your view of The Ten Commandments as either laws or love, religion or relationship, out-of-date or for you today ...

Part III (Days 61 – 90)

Welcome to Part 3 of 3. For the last 30 days, this guide will walk with you through INTERSECTION: *Divine Provision Meets Generosity Planning — How to Live Life to the Fullest While Richly Giving.*

Giving away God's Wealth is the most fun you can have with money. After I realized God owns everything, which I present in Part 2, it hit me: God gave to me so that I can give to others. Giving is exciting, but giving someone else's stuff is even more exhilarating. And, since God owns it all, and I really own nothing, that is the case every time I give.

This final part is all about why you should give, where to give, and how to give God's Wealth. You will learn to budget your way to larger and larger opportunities to give. I also share many ideas on how to give far beyond the amount of money in your bank account. It's part faith and part strategy, but all God's Wisdom.

These are not only Christian financial concepts and principles; these are financial truths. It's time for you to RECOVER, GROW, and ZERO IN on your financial target.

_____

_____

_____

_____

_____

_____

_____

_____

_____

_____

_____

_____

_____

_____

_____

_____

_____

Day 61

Reading:

- Introduction — Zero In On Giving
- Chapter 1 : God is a Giver — Intro
- Chapter 1 : God is a Giver — Generosity From the Beginning

Key Scripture:

But when thou doest alms, let not thy left hand know what thy right hand doeth: That thine alms may be in secret: and thy Father which seeth in secret himself shall reward thee openly (Matthew 6:3-4).

Questions:

- Do you feel that you are a giver by nature? Why or why not?_____

_____

_____

_____

_____

- List all the details of the very first gift God gave mankind?_____

_____

_____

_____

Journal about ...

... the ways you have given in the past ...

... the many attributes of God the Giver in your
life ...

_____

_____

_____

_____

_____

_____

_____

_____

_____

_____

_____

_____

_____

_____

_____

_____

_____

_____

_____

_____

_____

_____

Day 62

Reading:

Chapter 1 : God is a Giver — He Gave His All

Key Scripture:

For God so loved the world, that He gave His only begotten Son, that whosoever believeth in Him should not perish, but have everlasting life (John 3:16).

Questions:

• Why did God give His one and only Son?_____

_____

_____

_____

_____

_____

• In what ways did the good Samaritan give?_____

_____

_____

_____

_____

_____

Journal about ...

> ... your thankfulness for God's gift of salvation ...
> ... all the things you are thankful for that God has
> provided you and your family ...

_____

_____

_____

_____

_____

_____

_____

_____

_____

_____

_____

_____

_____

_____

_____

_____

_____

_____

_____

Day 63

Reading:

Chapter 1 : God is a Giver — He Keeps on
Giving

Key Scripture:

Since he did not spare even his own Son but gave him up
for us all, won't he also give us everything else?" (Romans
8:32 NLT)

Questions:

• Why is the Holy Spirit such a life changing gift?

_____

_____

_____

_____

_____

_____

• List the fruit of the Holy Spirit._____

_____

_____

_____

_____

_____

_____

Journal about ...

> ... the ways the fruit of the Holy Spirit have shaped your daily decisions and life events ...
>
> ... how you view eternal life in heaven as a gift ...

_____

_____

_____

_____

_____

_____

_____

_____

_____

_____

_____

_____

_____

_____

_____

_____

_____

_____

_____

_____

_____

Day 64

Reading:

- Chapter 2 : The Gift Received When Giving —
  Intro
- Chapter 2 : The Gift Received When Giving —
  The Gift You Get Today

Key Scripture:

Every generous act and every perfect gift is from above, coming down from the Father of lights (James 1:17a HCSB).

Questions:

- Why is it dangerous to give only to receive?_____

  _____

  _____

  _____

  _____

  _____

- What are some of the gifts you receive today when giving?_____

  _____

  _____

  _____

Journal about ...

> ... a time you were the recipient of a surprise gift
> from someone you didn't know ...
> ... ways you can give something small today ...

_____

_____

_____

_____

_____

_____

_____

_____

_____

_____

_____

_____

_____

_____

_____

_____

_____

_____

_____

_____

_____

Day 65

Reading:

Chapter 2 : The Gift Received When Giving —
The Gift You Get Tomorrow

Key Scripture:

Be ye therefore merciful, as your Father also is merciful.
Judge not, and ye shall not be judged: condemn not, and
ye shall not be condemned: forgive, and ye shall be
forgiven: Give, and it shall be given unto you; good
measure, pressed down, and shaken together, and running
over, shall men give into your bosom. For with the same
measure that ye mete withal it shall be measured to you
again (Luke 6:36-38).

Questions:

- How have other people impacted your life years
  after they gave to you?_____

  _____

  _____

- What are some of the gifts you receive tomorrow
  when giving today?_____

  _____

  _____

Journal about ...

... ways to be a giver with lasting effect ...

... how you can testify of God's promised return for giving ...

Day 66

Reading:

Chapter 2 : The Gift Received When Giving —
The Gift You Get Beyond Tomorrow

Key Scripture:

Lay not up for yourselves treasures upon earth, where moth and rust doth corrupt, and where thieves break through and steal: But **lay up for yourselves treasures in heaven**, where neither moth nor rust doth corrupt, and where thieves do not break through nor steal: **For where your treasure is, there will your heart be also** (Matthew 6:19-21).

Questions:

• How does giving your life to Christ change the way you live?_____

_____

_____

• What are some of the gifts you receive beyond tomorrow when giving?_____

_____

_____

Journal about ...

- ... a time when you did not give with the right motives ...
- ... the feelings, the sights, the experience of what heaven may be like to you ...

_____

_____

_____

_____

_____

_____

_____

_____

_____

_____

_____

_____

_____

_____

_____

_____

_____

_____

_____

_____

_____

_____

Day 67

Reading:

- Chapter 3 : Why Offerings? — Intro
- Chapter 3 : Why Offerings? — Obedience in Support

Key Scripture:

Every man **according as he purposeth in his heart**, so let him give; not grudgingly, or of necessity: for God loveth a cheerful giver (2 Corinthians 9:7).

Questions:

- Why does God desire for us to give offerings?___

  _____

  _____

  _____

  _____

- How should we come to God with our requests?

  _____

  _____

  _____

  _____

  _____

Journal about ...

... a time you gave an offering thinking more about how it will affect you than the impact it will have on others ...

... ways you can support your local church this year ...

Day 68

Reading:

Chapter 3 : Why Offerings? — To Honor and
Worship the Lord Your God

Key Scripture:

But I have all, and abound: I am full, having received of
Epaphroditus the things which were sent from you, an
odour of a sweet smell, a sacrifice acceptable, wellpleasing
to God (Philippians 4:18).

Questions:

• How does your giving honor God?_____

_____

_____

_____

_____

• Why did Jesus use parables surrounding financial
matters?_____

_____

_____

_____

_____

Journal about ...

... someone in the Bible who gave with the passion you want to pattern your giving after ...

... your thoughts about giving as worship ...

_____

_____

_____

_____

_____

_____

_____

_____

_____

_____

_____

_____

_____

_____

_____

_____

_____

_____

_____

_____

_____

_____

_____

_____

Day 69

Reading:

Chapter 3 : Why Offerings? — The Seriousness
of a Pledge

Key Scripture:

If a man vows a vow to the Lord, or swears an oath to bind
himself by a pledge, he shall not break his word. He shall
do according to all that proceeds out of his mouth
(Numbers 30:2 ESV).

Questions:

• Unless God has spoken to you otherwise, why
  should you wait to give until you are out of debt?

  _____

  _____

  _____

  _____

• What happens to you emotionally and spiritually
  when you don't honor your pledge?_____

  _____

  _____

  _____

Journal about ...

... any promises you have made but not been
faithful to ...

... how you will pray and plan the next time you
are presented an opportunity to support a
project or missionary ...

_____

_____

_____

_____

_____

_____

_____

_____

_____

_____

_____

_____

_____

_____

_____

_____

_____

_____

_____

Day 70

Reading:

- Chapter 4 : No Shame in Not Giving — Intro
- Chapter 4 : No Shame in Not Giving — Be Honest With Yourself

Key Scripture:

Instead of shame and dishonor, you will enjoy a double share of honor. You will possess a double portion of prosperity in your land, and everlasting joy will be yours (Isaiah 61:7 NLT).

Questions:

- Have you ever felt bad during a time when you could not afford to spend money on a gift?_____

_____

_____

_____

_____

- How does opportunity cost play a part in giving?

_____

_____

_____

_____

Journal about ...

... scriptures you will use to comfort your heart and
mind in order to combat shame ...

... ways you can honestly communicate with your
spouse about upcoming opportunities to give ...

_____

_____

_____

_____

_____

_____

_____

_____

_____

_____

_____

_____

_____

_____

_____

_____

_____

_____

_____

Day 71

Reading:

- Chapter 4 : No Shame in Not Giving — Be Honest With Others
- Chapter 4 : No Shame in Not Giving — It's Not a Competition

Key Scripture:

Let the eagerness you showed in the beginning be matched now by your giving. **Give in proportion to what you have.** Whatever you give is acceptable if you give it eagerly. And give according to what you have, not what you don't have. Of course, I don't mean your giving should make life easy for others and hard for yourselves. I only mean that there should be some equality. Right now you have plenty and can help those who are in need. Later, they will have plenty and can share with you when you need it. In this way, things will be equal. As the Scriptures say, "Those who gathered a lot had nothing left over, and those who gathered only a little had enough" (2 Corinthians 8:11b-15 NLT).

Questions:

- How does one justify giving more at some points in their life and giving little during other times?

_____

_____

_____

• What ways can you prevent holiday guilt before it has a chance to attack you?_____

_____

_____

_____

Journal about ...

... any toxic giving situations you may have experienced ...

... healthy boundaries you are going to enforce in your life going forward ...

_____

_____

_____

_____

_____

_____

_____

_____

_____

_____

_____

_____

_____

Day 72

Reading:

Chapter 4 : No Shame in Not Giving — Give For the Right Reasons

Key Scripture:

He will always make you rich enough to be generous at all times, so that many will thank God for your gifts which they receive from us (2 Corinthians 9:11 GNT).

Questions:

• What are some great reasons to give?_____

_____

_____

_____

_____

_____

• How has advertising played a part in promoting giving for the wrong reasons?_____

_____

_____

_____

_____

Journal about ...

... how you might modify your traditions during the Christmas season to course correct your family's giving mindset ...

... ways you will prioritize your giving opportunities throughout the year ...

_____

_____

_____

_____

_____

_____

_____

_____

_____

_____

_____

_____

_____

_____

_____

_____

_____

_____

_____

_____

Day 73

Reading:

- Chapter 5 : Give Without Spending a Penny — Intro
- Chapter 5 : Give Without Spending a Penny — How to Give Time

Key Scripture:

As we have therefore opportunity, let us do good unto all men, especially unto them who are of the household of faith (Galatians 6:10).

Questions:

- Why do we lean more towards gifts that cost money instead of non-monetary gifts?_____

_____

_____

_____

_____

- How is time more valuable than money?_____

_____

_____

_____

_____

_____

Journal about ...

... what it would feel like to go an entire year without giving something that costs money ...

... ways you can give of your time during Christmas this year ...

_____
_____
_____
_____
_____
_____
_____
_____
_____
_____
_____
_____
_____
_____
_____
_____
_____
_____
_____

Day 74

Reading:

Chapter 5 : Give Without Spending a Penny —
How to Give Hospitality

Key Scripture:

"Go and celebrate with a feast of rich foods and sweet drinks, and **share gifts of food with people who have nothing prepared**. This is a sacred day before our Lord. Don't be dejected and sad, for the joy of the Lord is your strength!" So the people went away to eat and drink at a festive meal, to **share gifts of food, and to celebrate with great joy** because they had heard God's words and understood them (Nehemiah 8:10,12 NLT).

Questions:

• What ways can you incorporate giving hospitality into your annual generosity plan?_____

_____

_____

_____

• If someone is an introvert, how could they still give the gift of hospitality?_____

_____

_____

_____

_____

Journal about ...

... a time you were given hospitality and the
thoughts you still reminisce about long after ...

... all the people in your neighborhood or city
who are in need of hospitality ...

_____

_____

_____

_____

_____

_____

_____

_____

_____

_____

_____

_____

_____

_____

_____

_____

_____

_____

_____

_____

_____

_____

Day 75

Reading:

- Chapter 5 : Give Without Spending a Penny —
  How to Give Talent
- Chapter 5 : Give Without Spending a Penny —
  These are the Most Cherished Gifts

Key Scripture:

As every man hath received the gift, even so minister the same one to another, as good stewards of the manifold grace of God (1 Peter 4:10).

Questions:

- How does giving time, hospitality, and talent have a lasting impact?_____

  _____

  _____

  _____

- Why do charitable organizations have more difficulty finding volunteers than donors?_____

  _____

  _____

  _____

Journal about ...

... that talent you have but don't think about because it comes so naturally ...

... ways you can use your talent to give for a birthday or wedding or any other opportunity coming up ...

_____

_____

_____

_____

_____

_____

_____

_____

_____

_____

_____

_____

_____

_____

_____

_____

_____

_____

_____

_____

Day 76

Reading:

- Chapter 6 : Give Without Spending A Lot — Intro
- Chapter 6 : Give Without Spending A Lot — Save Money While Being Generous

Key Scripture:

Take a lesson from the ants, you lazybones. Learn from their ways and become wise! Though they have no prince or governor or ruler to make them work, they labor hard all summer, gathering food for the winter (Proverbs 6:6-8 NLT).

Questions:

- How could one be irresponsible in managing God's wealth when it comes to giving gifts?_____

  _____

  _____

  _____

- What are three of the ways you can give without doing much shopping?_____

  _____

  _____

  _____

Journal about ...

   ... ways you could save money when going to the
   store to buy gifts ...
   ... things you have in a closet, in the basement, in
   the garage, ... going unused ...

_____

_____

_____

_____

_____

_____

_____

_____

_____

_____

_____

_____

_____

_____

_____

_____

_____

_____

_____

_____

_____

_____

Day 77

Reading:

- Chapter 6 : Give Without Spending A Lot — Reusing
- Chapter 6 : Give Without Spending A Lot — Repurposing

Key Scripture:

There is precious treasure and oil in the house of the wise [who prepare for the future], but a short-sighted and foolish man swallows it up and wastes it (Proverbs 21:20 AMP).

Questions:

- What techniques can you suggest to reuse or repurpose things to create a gift?_____

_____

_____

_____

- How could you think outside the gift-box, (i.e. having someone you know, who is super crafty, create something with your stuff that would make an incredible gift)?_____

_____

_____

_____

_____

Journal about ...

... a time you received an amazing gift that was handmade, and its value was far above the amount of money it most likely cost ...

... how you could reuse or repurpose items you listed on day 76 ...

_____

_____

_____

_____

_____

_____

_____

_____

_____

_____

_____

_____

_____

_____

_____

_____

Day 78

Reading:

Chapter 6 : Give Without Spending A Lot —
Regifting

Key Scripture:

Then Peter said, Silver and gold have I none; but such as I
have give I thee … (Acts 3:6a).

Questions:

- In what ways should regifting take time and
effort, though not much money?_____

_____

_____

_____

_____

- How could you take regifting to the next level by
combining it with garage sales / bargain hunting?

_____

_____

_____

_____

_____

Journal about ...

- ... a regifted item you have received and still cherish to this day ...
- ... what items you could regift from your list on day 76 ...

_____

_____

_____

_____

_____

_____

_____

_____

_____

_____

_____

_____

_____

_____

_____

_____

_____

_____

_____

_____

_____

_____

_____

Day 79

Reading:

- Chapter 7 : The Greatest Gifts You Could Ever Give — Intro
- Chapter 7 : The Greatest Gifts You Could Ever Give — The Gift Which Lasts Forever

Key Scripture:

The fruit of the righteous is a tree of life; and he that winneth souls is wise (Proverbs 11:30).

Questions:

- Why is sharing the gospel the greatest gift you could ever give? _____

  _____

  _____

  _____

- In what ways is leading someone to Christ regifting? _____

  _____

  _____

  _____

- Why is there no dollar amount that could compare to the gift of salvation? _____

  _____

_____

_____

Journal about ...

... how you could incorporate giving Jesus in your
work ...

... ways you could spend your leisure time to give
the greatest gifts you could ever give ...

... a time when you witnessed someone else
praying the sinner's prayer with someone else,
and how you felt as an onlooker ...

_____

_____

_____

_____

_____

_____

_____

_____

_____

_____

_____

_____

_____

_____

Day 80

Reading:

Chapter 7 : The Greatest Gifts You Could Ever
Give — The Gift Which Goes Unnoticed

Key Scripture:

The Scriptures say, "You must worship the Lord your God
and serve only him" (Luke 4:8 NLT).

Questions:

• How could you begin to serve in your home
  church?_____

  _____

  _____

  _____

  _____

• What is the reward for the things you do for
  others that go unnoticed?_____

  _____

  _____

  _____

  _____

  _____

Journal about ...

... the blessings you receive at the INTERSECTION of worship and service ...

... ways you could serve your community ...

_____

_____

_____

_____

_____

_____

_____

_____

_____

_____

_____

_____

_____

_____

_____

_____

_____

_____

_____

_____

Day 81

Reading:

Chapter 7 : The Greatest Gifts You Could Ever
Give — The Gift Which Originates in the Closet

Key Scripture:

I exhort therefore, that, first of all, **supplications,
prayers, intercessions, and giving of thanks, be made
for all men**; for kings, and for all that are in authority; that
we may lead a quiet and peaceable life in all godliness and
honesty. For this is good and acceptable in the sight of
God our Saviour; who will have all men to be saved, and to
come unto the knowledge of the truth. **For there is one
God, and one mediator between God and men, the
man Christ Jesus; who gave himself a ransom for all,
to be testified in due time** (1 Timothy 2:1-6).

Questions:

• What is the definition of intercession?_____

_____

_____

_____

• How can prayer be the most time intensive gift
  of all?_____

_____

_____

_____

Journal about ...

... the thought that someone is spending their time to pray for you and things that have happened (or not happened) as a result of those prayers ...

... all the people in your life who you could spend time praying for today ...

_____

_____

_____

_____

_____

_____

_____

_____

_____

_____

_____

_____

_____

_____

_____

_____

_____

Day 82

Reading:

- Chapter 8 : Where Giving Fits into the Budget — Intro
- Chapter 8 : Where Giving Fits into the Budget — Giving Fund is a Sinking Fund

Key Scripture:

But generous people plan to do what is generous, and they stand firm in their generosity (Isaiah 32:8 NLT).

Questions:

- How does budgeting allow you to be more generous?_____

  _____

  _____

  _____

  _____

- What is the definition of a sinking fund?_____

  _____

  _____

  _____

  _____

Journal about ...

- ... how past giving moments would have been less stressful if you had a budget ...
- ... the different areas in your money management where you can create a sinking fund ...

_____

_____

_____

_____

_____

_____

_____

_____

_____

_____

_____

_____

_____

_____

_____

_____

_____

_____

_____

_____

_____

Day 83

Reading:

Chapter 8 : Where Giving Fits into the Budget —
Giving Occasions Are Not Emergencies

Key Scripture:

Be thou diligent to know the state of thy flocks, and look
well to thy herds (Proverbs 27:23).

Questions:

- How do people get fooled into going into debt in
  the name of generosity?_____

  _____

  _____

  _____

  _____

- What role does opportunity cost play in a wise
  financial generosity plan?_____

  _____

  _____

  _____

  _____

  _____

Download the Gift Giving Planner template from the resource page here: intersection.zeroinfinancial.com

Journal about ...

... ways you can avoid using your emergency fund for gifts ...

... future dates and times for planning financial obligations and giving opportunities ...

Day 84

Reading:

- Chapter 8 : Where Giving Fits into the Budget
  — Think Long Term When It Comes to Kid's
  Gifts
- Chapter 8 : Where Giving Fits into the Budget
  — Divide and Conquer

Key Scripture:

Owe nothing to anyone—except for your obligation to love one another (Romans 13:8a).

Questions:

- How has the written letter become a special gift today?_____

  _____

  _____

  _____

  _____

- What are various methods to divide and conquer for giving during Christmas?_____

  _____

  _____

  _____

  _____

Journal about ...

... ways you can give to the kids in your life by thinking long term ...

... a group gift you have received which made you feel loved ...

Day 85

Reading:

- Chapter 9 : Three Ways to Give — Intro
- Chapter 9 : Three Ways to Give — Regular Gifts and Offerings

Key Scripture:

I beseech you therefore, brethren, by the mercies of God, that ye present your bodies a living sacrifice, holy, acceptable unto God, which is your reasonable service (Romans 12:1).

Questions:

- What are some of the times of regular gifts and offerings?_____

_____

_____

_____

_____

- How can you give yourself as a gift?_____

_____

_____

_____

_____

Download the Gift Giving Planner template from the resource page:
zeroinfinancial.com/intersection

Journal about ...

... ways you can plan for regular times of giving ...

... how you will avoid overloading your gift giving plan ...

Day 86

Reading:

Chapter 9 : Three Ways to Give — Spontaneous Gifts

Key Scripture:

Watch therefore: for ye know not what hour your Lord doth come (Matthew 24:42).

Questions:

• How can you make sure to be sensitive to the voice of the Lord when it comes to spontaneous giving?_____

_____

_____

_____

_____

• What can you do to be prepared for others' needs at random times?_____

_____

_____

_____

_____

Journal about ...

- ... a time when you had an emergency and someone was generous to you in your hour of need ...
- ... your game plan when you desire to give more than you have ...

_____

_____

_____

_____

_____

_____

_____

_____

_____

_____

_____

_____

_____

_____

_____

_____

_____

_____

_____

Day 87

Reading:

Chapter 9 : Three Ways to Give — Outrageous
Gifts

Key Scripture:

Sell your possessions and give to those in need. This will
store up treasure for you in heaven! And the purses of
heaven never get old or develop holes. Your treasure will
be safe; no thief can steal it and no moth can destroy it
(Luke 12:33).

Questions:

• In what ways could someone give that could be
considered outrageous?_____

_____

_____

_____

_____

• Why does extreme giving take 90% faith and 10%
strategy?_____

_____

_____

_____

Journal about ...

- ... your thoughts and prayers concerning outrageous generosity ...
- ... how you are preparing your life and financial plan to be ready for any giving opportunity ...

_____

_____

_____

_____

_____

_____

_____

_____

_____

_____

_____

_____

_____

_____

_____

_____

_____

_____

_____

Day 88

Reading:

- Chapter 10 : More Examples of Giving in the Word of God — Intro
- Chapter 10 : More Examples of Giving in the Word of God — Purpose Driven Giving

Key Scripture:

And when they were come into the house, they saw the young child with Mary his mother, and fell down, and worshipped him: and **when they had opened their treasures, they presented unto him gifts; gold, and frankincense, and myrrh"** (Matthew 2:11).

Questions:

- What is Purpose Driven Giving?_____

  _____

  _____

  _____

  _____

- Why were the gifts from the three wise men so special?_____

  _____

  _____

  _____

Journal about ...

... how you will seek God's purpose in your gift giving ...

... a time when you received a gift into which someone put a lot of thought and prayer ...

_____

_____

_____

_____

_____

_____

_____

_____

_____

_____

_____

_____

_____

_____

_____

_____

_____

_____

_____

_____

_____

_____

Day 89

Reading:

- Chapter 10 : More Examples of Giving in the Word of God — Prosperity Driven Giving
- Chapter 10 : More Examples of Giving in the Word of God — Passion Driven Giving

Key Scripture:

And they spake unto Moses, saying, The people bring much more than enough for the service of the work, which the Lord commanded to make (Exodus 36:3-7).

Questions:

- What is Prosperity Driven Giving?_____

_____

_____

_____

- What is Passion Driven Giving?_____

_____

_____

_____

- In what ways was David's offering, in 2 Samuel Chapter 24, full of passion?_____

_____

_____

Journal about ...

... someone who gave a extraordinary gift because they had worked hard and positioned themselves to be used in this way ...

... a situation, a charity, a cause, ... that you're passionate about supporting ...

Day 90

Reading:

- Chapter 10 : More Examples of Giving in the Word of God — Provision Driven Giving
- Chapter 10 : More Examples of Giving in the Word of God — Power Driven Giving
- Conclusion — Because You Have Given

Key Scripture:

Neither was there any among them that lacked: for as many as were possessors of lands or houses sold them, and brought the prices of the things that were sold, And laid them down at the apostles' feet: and distribution was made unto every man according as he had need (Acts 4:34-35).

Questions:

- What is Provision Driven Giving?_____

  _____

  _____

  _____

- What is Power Driven Giving?_____

  _____

  _____

  _____

- Why did Jesus give the gift from the young boy to the disciples to give again to the people?

Journal about ...

... how you would feel if there was a unity and sharing in your community as it was with the first church in Acts ...

... a time when God performed a miracle through you for someone else's need ...

... the names of God you could call on when seeking guidance during generosity planning ...

Well Done!

Congratulations! You've completed 90 days of reading, studying, and meditating on God's Word. Now you can create a financial strategy backed by faith in your Heavenly Father. You can manage money from the proper perspective of the Owner-Steward INTERSECTION. And you are ready to be generous like never before as God so graciously blesses you with more to give away.

Since you have been raised to new life with Christ,
set your sights on the realities of heaven,
where Christ sits in the place of honor
at God's right hand. — Colossians 3:1 NLT

Now that you have set your sights on the INTERSECTION, don't stop there. After "ready", "aim", and "focus" comes "fire"! It's time to hit your financial target with accuracy. Applying these truths takes daily practice, so make sure to stay tightly in communication with your accountability partner, budget consistently, and give all the way to the day you hear those sweet words: "Well Done!"

So, go zero in on your financial target at the INTERSECTION where God's Wealth meets God's Wisdom.

Remember to visit the Resource page, where there are many helpful tools today that will continually grow with new and updated guides, here:

intersection.zeroinfinancial.com

Free Resources

To help you Zero In on the INTERSECTION where God's Wealth meets God's Wisdom, download the free resources from the INTERSECTION Resource Page:

intersection.zeroinfinancial.com

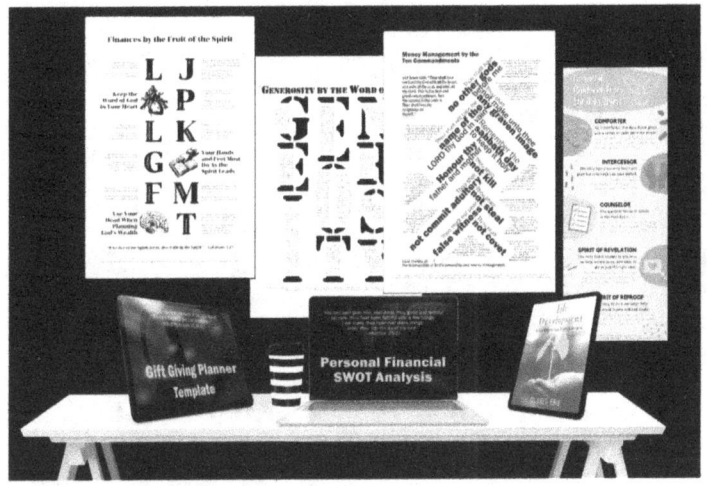

- **BOOK:** Life Development—A New Believer's Guide to Growing in Christ

- **INFOGRAPHIC:** Financial Guidance from the Holy Spirit

- **POSTER:** Finances by the Fruit of the Spirit

- **WORKBOOK:** Personal Financial SWOT Analysis

- **POSTER:** Money Management by the Ten Commandments

- **WORKBOOK:** Gift Giving Planner Template

- **POSTER:** Generosity by the Word of God

Thank You!

To all those who have been so generous to financially support the creation of this book series, I am so thankful. You helped bring INTERSECTION to fruition.

Forward Church Myrtle Beach
Kuba Wyrobek
Clovers & Val McWilliams
Carlos & Maria Correa
Ellie Markova
Anton & Aleksandra Zhloba
Pastor Chris, Heather, & Nelson Honeycutt
Dr. Anthony Jenkins
Pastor Allen & Debbie Causey
D.S. & Stella Wilson
D. Greg & Susie Ebie
David & Kelly Franco
Nicholas Ryan Rendleman
Kaffa Morales
Scott Petrarca
Marcos & Mireya Bernal
Angel Christopher
Pastor Steve & Jessica Mueller
Nick Kolovos
Anibal & Joelia Maldonado
David Gumins
J. Varghese
Linda Ostrowski
Steve & Traci Hickman
Richard L. Dobbins, Jr.
Pastor Edgar & Christie Rivas
Christian Baird
John Kuntharayil
Vuong Dinh
Chaplain James F. Burling
Adele van der Lecq
Edgar Rios

Note from the Author: Reviews are gold to authors! If you have enjoyed this book, would you consider reviewing it on your favorite book retailer's website? Thank you!

About the Author

Johnny McWilliams, founder of Zero In Financial LLC, guides his students, customers, and clients as they RECOVER from past money mistakes, GROW your present pocketbook position, and ZERO IN on your future financial fortune, ultimately leaving a lasting legacy of love. After working as a tax preparer, dissecting the details of credit scoring and reporting, passing various exams and licensure, including Series 7, Series 66, life & health insurance, and real estate broker, Johnny realized the average American's need for financial coaching, education, and inspiration.

Once Johnny completed ten years of enlistment in the United States Navy, graduated with a Master of Business Administration, worked as a property & casualty insurance consultant, and became certified as a Ramsey Solutions Master Financial Coach, he began guiding individuals and families to Zero In on their financial target.

Johnny and his wife, Christine, have been married for over twelve years, and they are blessed with one married son, one married daughter, and no grandchildren yet.